Home of Sudden Service

HOME OF
SUDDEN SERVICE

ELIZABETH BACHINSKY

NIGHTWOOD EDITIONS
ROBERTS CREEK, BC
2006

Nightwood Editions
R.R. #22, 3692 Beach Ave.
Roberts Creek, BC, Canada V0N 2W2
www.nightwoodeditions.com

Edited by Kathy Sinclair

Nightwood Editions acknowledges the financial support of the Government of Canada through the Canada Council for the Arts and the Book Publishing Industry Development Program (BPIDP), and from the Province of British Columbia through the British Columbia Arts Council, for its publishing activities.

Printed and bound in Canada.

LIBRARY AND ARCHIVES CANADA CATALOGUING IN PUBLICATION

Bachinsky, Elizabeth, 1976-
    Home of sudden service / Elizabeth Bachinsky.

Poems.
ISBN 0-88971-212-3

    I. Title.

PS8603.A33H65 2006   C811'.6   C2005-907206-7

For my family

Contents

9 Valley

VALLEY GIRLS

13 Pack

14 Of a Time

16 St. Sarah

19 For the Teen Moms at the Valley Fair Mall

23 How to Bag Your Small-Town Girl

24 Home of Sudden Service

26 Wolf Lake

28 Night Voices

29 For the Pageant Girls: Miss Teen Motel 6 et al.

31 SOMETIMES BOYS GO MISSING

VALLEY GIRLS LOVE VALLEY BOYS

45 Wild Grass

46 Of a Place

47 Outcasts

49 For the Punk Rock Boys

50 At Fifteen

51 St. Michael

53 Petit Mal, Petit Mort

54 To a Future Delinquent

55 B&E

56 Mary Hill

57 Near Miss

58 The Diner of Her Heart

59 DRIVE

77 Acknowledgements

VALLEY

Yours is the landscape of my youth: freeways
superb in all their trash and glam. Your
cold suburban cartography
falls where it falls, like breathing, or wind.
Your faults are mine and mine
yours. When we kiss, you light my Vacancy.
Yours is the trailer park fire of the mind,
a vinyl-sided wet dream: Kathie Lee
meets corned beef hash, the scream of a swing set
rusty from years of schoolyard piss and shit.
Jesus, I long for you each moment
I'm away. I want your legs as far apart
as the poles. Sick, I'm sick with longing for
some punk midnight vandal, some bleach-blonde hair.

Valley Girls

PACK

We learned to sell ourselves early in life. Got badges
for good sales and how to sew. The deft among us praised
for the perfect square knot, we chanted, feverishly
fumbling, *Right over left, left over right and under…*

Polite, our socks yanked tight up under our knees,
we made vows to the Queen. We really meant them.
Our secret hand signals, our hierarchy,
we were like the Freemasons, only smaller.

We were made to circle a mushroom. Not sure why.
The moms, let's not forget the moms—
automatons, pre-programmed to pick up
and drop off and pick up again.

O, they'd crowd in the corner of the gym
unable to pick out their kid from a distance.
All that competition! *Here, here! Over here!*
you'd scream—as if screaming would set you apart.

Later, we would be waitresses, work in factories.
Sell beautiful things we ourselves could not afford.
Later, we'd bury our mothers—every one of us.
Plant mushrooms in the dirt. Circle them.

OF A TIME

When the voices of children are heard on the green
And laughing is heard on the hill,
My heart is at rest within my breast
And everything else is still.

William Blake, "Nurse's Song," *Songs of Innocence*

Here is the place where I grew up:
a ridge of high cold mountain surrounds
a flat town set deep
into a valley. Thirty thousand
people live here, three of them
my own. I am lucky; we keep horses:
two big bays with quick eyes
and soft coats that gleam when I brush them.
I have friends. I bridle my animal
and ride out to meet them. Together, we ride
over pastures into the pale forest light.
Our galloping: our bodies' thrilled moment,
staunch cedars whipped into a green haze,
our paths chopped to bits by hooves.
Now, into the ravine, we lean back
in our saddles, feel our muscles
heat with strain as our horses' haunches dig in
to the bank. We go down, feet thrust
firm in our stirrups as we hit the muddy
water and then—we are light!

Is it possible that such a beast can swim?
He weighs a ton (at least!) but here
he is, his expectant ears pricked forward,
forward, as he glides through the murk.
The trees have made a room for us,
surround our sounds, the sounds of girls
swimming with horses.
How far we are from the town. How
we animate ourselves.

ST. SARAH

I

Sarah was a dyke. We all knew it from
the way she wore her hair short, tucked under
a baseball cap, and kissed Fran's sister whether
she wanted to be kissed or not. Whatever. When
you're a kid, you do things—stick fingers in
holes to feel for fur. There are things a
kid needs to touch. So we did. Like when Sarah
got me alone and we touched tongues on
the chesterfield. A wet welcoming
gesture. Quick, like an animal, she slipped
her arms around me, tilted back my head—
like this, she said, and kissed me. Thrilling
moment, and then—nothing. No tripped
alarm. No sudden love for her, no sudden dread.

II

The truth is—that never happened. Sarah
never kissed me on the sly. There is no
Sarah. I lied. You really want to know
the truth? I'll have to take you back to my first
hometown, a northern place where it's cold
as hell and the girls are straight as lodgepole pines.
You couldn't get a peek or a peck if you tried.
I was shy, but loved many. The hands I held
were my own on freezing nights, skating poorly
around the outdoor rink my parents poured
with the neighbours. That was me, chased home
by the grocer's boys, who taunted relentlessly
you fat-ass, you fatty, as if I were some
dumb animal, and counted on to be a coward.

III

Ha! If I were ten again I would be
Sarah, a girl so smart, a girl so tough
you wouldn't mess with her, not even to cough
in her direction. If you called *her* fatty,
well, fuck it, she wouldn't care. *Who are*
those assholes anyway? she'd say. *Fuck 'em.*
Sarah who'd tame a wild Arabian
stallion and ride him through the rainforest, bare-
backed without a bit. Who'd have the key
to every city and a swart red ship in which
she'd sail every lake and every ocean—
twice. She who'd tame barracudas: an army
of voracious fish. O, if I were ten
again, I'd be Sarah. Do not doubt this.

FOR THE TEEN MOMS AT THE VALLEY FAIR MALL

1: Jenni

The first time Jenni had sex, she was thirteen and the
condom broke inside her and she thought: I have AIDS,
even though the boy on whom the prophylactic snapped
had never known a girl in that sense before, and when he saw
the sad, deflated thing at the end of his prick he still gave
a push at her slit, no idea he'd unwrapped
the candy, so to speak. And so she lived that way for days,
thinking: I have AIDS, when really she was pregnant, a days-
old zygote swimming among her veins—the fast
dread of her sickness so palpable that when she gave
birth, at last, she tried to push it back.

2: Sez Jenni

Truth is, when his hands were on me, I was fire.
Straight through to my gut, I felt my heart beat
in my body like heavy metal, that oh
baby kind of get-your-hard-on-over-here
loving I'd only heard of at lunch in the smoke pit
at school—tough girls running off their mouths
so hard you're sure they must be lying: cock this
and fuck that: it's all so unbelievable, isn't it—
the things girls say? But, let me tell you, when his smooth
talk comes, their chatter fades away. There is only:
his pink mouth.

3: Bungee

Some girls know they want it early on:
the husband, the kids, the whole freak circus sideshow
of diaper bags and diapers, dentist's and doctor's appointments.
So when Sarah, at fifteen, and for the fourth time, took a good long
pee on a white plastic stick, and it turned its peacock hue,
bright blue in her mother's bathroom under the cool fluorescents,
she felt her heart go quick, a feeling of falling
matched only by the time she'd gone toes-
up off the edge of a bridge in North Vancouver. That same tense
feeling as before she'd jumped, in the waiting
for her blue consequence.

4: And furthermore

when you have a kid too soon, they send you to
a special "class" at school where you learn
some things the other girls don't learn, sometimes, ever:
how to change a diaper, how to test a bottle (too cool
is bad for the baby's stomach and too hot may burn
his mouth) or what to do when your daughter's fever
reaches 102, which is helpful, but not helpful when you're trying
to picture exactly how to study math with a newborn
boy… or how you'll tell your boyfriend he's a father,
or what you'll do when that boyfriend freezes over,
and his loving is over.

HOW TO BAG YOUR SMALL-TOWN GIRL

Those small-town girls they like to marry early
you know. Can't wait to settle down, have
a kid or two. What they wouldn't give
for a solid man, one who's ready
to rein it in—that rampant prick—and stick
close to home, a good father, provider
and lover, a tall drink of water
who's cool when the pickup's bust, stick
shift stuck in second gear or the condom's broke
again. But there's no such thing as too much man
to handle. Those girls, they like them rough
around the edges, tough boys who'll never balk
at next month's rent with heart enough to love
a woman right, again and again and again.

HOME OF SUDDEN SERVICE

The last year of high school, I got a job
as a pizza delivery person, drove burning hot
stacks of Hawaiian-with-extra-cheese around
all night in my Volkswagen Rabbit. The radio
always playing something like "Smoke
on the Water" or "Crazy on You," and I smoked
so many cigarettes my pointer finger started
turning really yellow. After a while, they let me work
in the kitchen too. Squirting bottles of sweet
tomato sauce onto discs of dough.
I quit that place for the coffee shop with
the medical/dental and got an apartment
with Angel right away, which was about time.
The first month, we made love
in every room. I worked my ass
off in the coffee shop and got myself promoted
to shift supervisor after only four months;
Angel got on full-time at the shop.
So I got my Dogwood and I got pregnant.
Didn't seem to be any reason not to, especially
with the mat leave, and we weren't wrong.
Cole's three-and-a-half now. I have to leave him
with Mom on the days I go to work.
I try to get a lot of early shifts so I can spend
nights with Angel and Cole, but it's hard.
There aren't that many supervisors at the shop,

so I have to work a lot of nights anyway.
It's a lot of responsibility. On my days off
I take Cole to visit his dad at work.
Cole loves a truck up on a jack.
Whenever we show up, we wait for Angel
in the office. There's a sign out front that reads
Home of Sudden Service, but sometimes
it takes him a while to notice us.
When he looks out from under the truck
and sees us, though, he gives
us this shy kind of smile, as if we're his secret
and heat passes through my body like a wave.
Sometimes I think he's still getting used
to the idea of us. When he comes home, he's filthy,
but I love the smell of him, he smells like my father
used to when he came home from work.
I don't know… is that fucked up? I don't think so.

WOLF LAKE

It was down that road he brought me, still
in the trunk of his car. I won't say it felt right,
but it did feel expected. The way you know
your blood can spring like a hydrant.
That September, the horseflies were murder
in the valley. I'd come home to visit the family,
get in a couple of weeks of free food, hooked up
with a guy I'd known when I was a kid and things
went bad. When he cut me, I remember
looking down, my blood surprising as paper
snakes leaping from a tin. He danced me
around his basement apartment, dumped me
on the chesterfield, sat down beside me, and lit
a smoke. He seemed a black bear in the gloam,
shoulders rounded under his clothes,
so I tried to remember everything I knew
about black bears: *whistle while you walk… carry bells…*
if you don't bother them, they won't bother you…
play dead. Everything slowed. I'll tell you a secret.
It's hard to kill a girl. You've got to cut her bad
and you've got to cut her right, and the boy had done neither.
Pain rose along the side of my body, like light.
I lay very still while he smoked beside me: this boy
I'd camped with every summer since we were twelve,
the lake so quiet you could hear the sound
of a heron skim the water at dusk, or the sound
of a boy's breathing. I came-to in the trunk of his car,
gravel kicking up against the frame, dust coming in

through the cracks. It was dark. I was thirsty.
I couldn't move my hands or legs,
The pain was still around. I think I was tied.
We drove that way for a long time before
the Chrysler finally slowed, then stopped. Sound
of gravel crunching under tires. I could smell the lake,
a place where, as kids, we'd come to swim
and know we'd never be seen. Logs grew
up from that lakebed. All those black bones
rising from black water. I remember,
we'd always smelled of lake water and of sex
by the end of the day, and there was a tape of Patsy
Cline we always liked to sing to on our way out—
which is what I thought we'd be doing that September
afternoon. That, or smoking up in his garage.

You know, you hear about the Body
all the time: *They found the Body…*
the Body was found… and then you are one.
Someone once told me the place had been
a valley, before the dam, before the town.
But that was a long time ago. When the engine stopped,
I heard the silver sound of keys in the lock
and then I was up on his shoulders, tasting blood.
I think he said my name. I think he walked
toward the woods.

NIGHT VOICES

I want the chilled blue
nights I gave to girls I'll never see again.
I want their long cool limbs,
the faint movement their bodies made beside me,
rain on the flysheet of our tent, a lake below
us, dark and quiet, but for night
birds—bats—hurtling through the bent
branches above. I want my girls back-
lit by the moon then warmed
by the campfire we built together.
I want their secrets. To hear
their high laughter from a distance
among the trees, so far from the houses where
we lived, we felt free.

FOR THE PAGEANT GIRLS:
MISS TEEN MOTEL 6, ET AL.

We met when we were young enough to know
each street, and side street, of our town by name.
That beauty changes us and why and how

becomes apparent when you live below
a mountain. What was its name again?
We met when we were young enough to know.

This is what we saw from our windows:
a parking lot, a dollar store, rain.
That beauty could change us and why and how

seemed unjust. Unfair! What did we know
but that our loves seemed dull and strange.
We met when we were young enough to know

we'd move to far-off places. We had hopes
to find ourselves on MTV, so certain
beauty could change us. Why and how

seemed unimportant, as long as we'd just go.
So some left, some didn't; all of us changed.
We met when we were young enough to know
that beauty could change us—not why or how.

Sometimes Boys
Go Missing

I

(Prologue)

It's when the handmade posters go up, you know
desperation. That crude lettering. The family

kicking themselves they've only got the Polaroid
from Christmas three years back, and that one's none

too good. That why-didn't-we-keep-better-track talk
and staples stuck in telephone poles, Xerox gone

to tatters after one good rain. That can't-make-out-
his-face-anymore-the-sun's-gone-bleached-it-out

decoupage / paper pileup where his face once was
on the corkboard at the grocery store.

That cop-shop's-given-up-but-we've-got-Jesus-uptown
touch-of-hope you see papering and papering your town.

II

In this story, a boy drives out to an airport,

a small local airport. The kind of airport where boys
with moneyed parents learn to fly small planes.

                              Small planes,
because that's all this landing strip can handle

and the business of teaching boys to transport goods from small
town to small town likes to remain small and unnoticed.

What a pretty area: vast tracts of lush grass along a river.
There are multicoloured parachutes on the horizon.

       small   small

          small

             small

                 small

          small

III

Perhaps, having approached the airstrip, the boy pulled
his little Dodge into the long grass at the side of the road.

It was a very blue day in the middle
of what the boy's mother liked to call an Indian summer –

so it was hot. Hotter than usual for that time of year.
In this story, the boy takes the airport road

as respite from the heat of the day and our principal
player, one gift-wrapped something, is a gift

for his girlfriend who, blonde, twenty-seven,
a mental health worker for social services, gives fabulous head.

He thinks of this as the car shudders to a halt
at the roadside and he lifts his keys from the ignition:

of how terrific soft her mouth feels on the length of him.
Lovely thought to have in the middle of an Indian

summer on the last day before this trusting boy
leaves his doors unlocked to take a walk to the cool arm

of the Fraser for a dip under the deciduous, slips
on the muddy bank, cracks his head on a stone and drifts away

   downstream.

IV

    …look, I knew the guy. He spent his time
in the parking lots of pubs drinking from the lip of a paper bag

and hanging off the gate of his dad's pickup. In those moments,
we said, hey, we've licked some pussy, which was true

or not true depending on who you talked to and on which day
of the week—and once he even almost nearly died from a fall

he took off the back of the thing after Jordie,
who had never driven stick shift, put the truck in gear

and bunny-hopped a foot or two before he went
and put it in the ditch. After that we always said

Ha! That was a night to remember….

V

                    But, you know,
there have always been rumours of cult activity near this river,
and the rumours make sense if you think about them long enough.
                    Think: a dark covering

of trees late at night, the smell of soft green fermentation
and gasoline, the river delivering its detritus like a muscled arm.

Think about a boy, vanished, twenty-eight, who left no note, no
nothing, just a gift-wrapped something (they won't say what)

as dead weight on the passenger seat, almost certainly
hoping for someone to find it.

VI

He couldn't fly a fucking plane. He was no rich boy
fly boy. Fuck that. He could barely drive a car.

Here's what I think, for what it's worth:
How many shots does a boy have to shoot
before he drinks himself

to death? You want to find that boy, you drag that river.
You don't find him then, you drag English Bay.

By now his body's just a cage. But, you know,
they've got dental records, right?

Mostly it just makes me sick, your conspiracy
theories. Like you've got to have a reason. Well,
sometimes there isn't a reason. Sometimes boys go missing.

And what did he leave me... some lousy underwear?
Fuck your rumours. I want what's mine,
but the police won't say a word.

VII

                              Or perhaps his plane
ploughed through the cumulus cloud cover. His little car
a fleck below.

        Alpha, Bravo, Charlie, Delta, Echo, Foxtrot, etc… etc…
and the boy used the landscape as his guide:

mountains to the north, fields to the east, ocean to the west.
                              Vast muddy river to the south.

Perhaps he knew how in the fall salmon writhe their way
through this silt-rich river to bump heads with the ancient
fish who live there all year round.

Perhaps he knew, when the salmon speak, they say,
                              Just passing through.
How the old ones answer, *Keep it moving keep it moving.*

So he did.

VIII

(in a voice distorted so as to become unrecognizable)

It was beautiful, the efficiency with which our operation
functioned toward the end. Eventually we had boys
picking up and dropping off for they couldn't tell you why
    or where.

They were like Pavlov's dogs—that's plural, kid.
It's a beautiful thing, the wiped-out mind.

Nothing's cleaner than nothing.

In this story, the boy takes the airport road
because we told him to. And that principal player,
that gift-wrapped something?

Underwear for the girlfriend. A red herring.
And we put that there too.

Last I saw the boy he was loading twenty-kilo floursacks
    into a Cessna
bound for Alert Bay. The kind of boy who could lift the things
    like they were nothing.

IX

(Epilogue)

…I remember once he said he'd rather cut off his own arm
         than kill a man

and I believed him.

He was the kind of guy you could trust with your life
and your girlfriend,

that's all I know.

That and I never got back the router I lent him
to do the edging on his mom's new kitchen cabinets.

              It's a damn shame
what happened to him.

What happened to him?

He was a good guy to have a beer with.

Anyway, the router's gone.

Valley Girls Love
Valley Boys

WILD GRASS

How easily we are transformed. For some
it takes only a lover's hand moving like water

through their hair—the shushing of a voice to shape them.
From that moment, living has reversed itself. *Now*, they say,

I will work my way back towards birth rather than from it.
This is misfortune, or fortune, depending on where you stand.

But think. At first a man's body is too much to bear.
There is too much of it, and all of it strange—strange

as another country, another gravity. His love first sounds
like labour, like pleasure, and somehow you know it is both.

This weight is how we begin. Like wild grass
from under the hoof of a pastured animal, we spring up.

OF A PLACE

When the voices of children are heard on the green
And whisp'rings are in the dale,
The days of my youth rise fresh in my mind
My face turns green and pale.

William Blake, "Nurse's Song," *Songs of Experience*

Please see the town from above.
It is flat. Note the grid-work. Pick
a road, any road. (It doesn't matter which).
I am three days late and failing French
9 for the second time. I eat speed
and tweak through PE. A boy waits for me
by the bus stop. I know his hunched shape,
his too-wide shoulders, how he pulls them down, pulls
his hands into his sleeves as if he could hide
his size. He's too big to be a boy,
but he's a boy. Some nights we climb onto the roof
outside his bedroom window, drink his parents' MGD
while they watch TV in the family room.
I like his cruel eyes, his punk rock hair.
I like his parents. How they pretend not to hear
our sounds at three AM—him and me so drunk,
I have to cut his boots off with a knife.

OUTCASTS

Search out the early misfit who at school,
sickly for love and giddy with his sex
found friendship like a door banged in his face,
his world a wasteland and himself a fool.

P.K. Page, "Outcasts"

Across your halls, your double-wide classrooms,
stood gangs of boys in hooded sweatshirts,
jeans and T-shirts artfully arranged
to maximize their apathetic charm
or, perhaps, the leanness of their arms
and backs, their heavy-lidded eyes too full
of your body to ignore: fervent boys
whose gazes promised lecherous intent
and afternoons of fumbled love. But to
search out the early misfit… who at school

among us had such courage? He stood
in his own shadow, his brow a constant line
across his face. You will remember him
as you knew him: not at all, though,
he watched you with the haunted eyes
of a scolded child from the rim of his math text-
book, read the lines your body made under
your clothes. How desperately he loved the
long pale hair that fell to your back like flax,
sickly for love and giddy with his sex;

and yet, his hangdog looks did nothing to
inspire your love. You didn't see, but he
still saw, saw how at night you lay beneath
those undeserving boys, despair rising
in his throat. How could he speak? Too shy
to even say your name aloud or place
his hand beside your hand, he had no words
for what he had to say, and you were gone
besides, too high to care if he, enraged,
found friendship like a door banged in his face.

I tell you, seek him out—or one as like
as you can find; and if he's grown enough
to take your hand, I tell you: give it up.
If you still feel, after all that you have felt,
let go your faux sophistication.
Embrace him. If he unravels like a spool
of thread, so much the better to remind
you of your own pent need. Tell him again
the story of the years you did at school
your world a wasteland, and yourself a fool.

FOR THE PUNK ROCK BOYS

The stars engraved your names indelibly
as ink under my skin, you valley boys:
Sean and Shaun and Michael, Paul and Steve.

How often fifty fingers tried to free
my half-formed breasts on nights you boys,
like stars, engraved your names indelibly

with knives into the bark of a pine tree
or a park bench. The parks filled with your noise.
Sean and Shaun and Michael, Paul and Steve,

how strange you were, above me—strange like thieves
one frightens in a heist. You were just boys
with stars engraved, like names, indelibly

along your boyish veins. You stood out green
under your flesh. You tasted like a choice.
Sean and Shaun and Michael, Paul and Steve,

you wore your anger as you wore your need,
as politic or fashion, such little joy—
and yet, the stars inscribed your names. *Indelibly,*
Sean and Shaun and Michael, Paul and Steve.

AT FIFTEEN
after Irving Layton

Their chests like planks, bellies
like planks,
I want to undress boys
as a carpenter undresses

a block of pine.
Their clothes, shed like shavings,
smell of aftershave, of pine.
I want them naked, contrapposto,

still as posts. They are so polished
beneath their shirts and jeans.
They are so lean, penises
rearing, eager, impatient as ponies.

Young men: all edges, jut of hip, whip of spine.
What temperamental instruments they are,
what clichéd agonies they moan,
my mouth on them now
and then gone.

ST. MICHAEL

And in my heart there stirs a quiet pain
For unremembered lads that not again
Will turn to me at midnight with a cry.

Edna St. Vincent Millay

Once, I slept with this guy
from work. His name was
Michael. He was seventeen,
and I wasn't much
older. I brought him
home with me after
a shift at the coffee shop
where we'd been
squirting whipped cream
on top of mochas
for eight hours or so.
He didn't want to spend
the night. Didn't want
to upset his mom who was
waiting for him to come
home—which was fine
with me. He came;
I leaned onto my elbow,
looked over at him, and he
sighed
just like in Millay's poem,
so we did it again. He tasted

sweet, like something you'd stir
into your coffee.
He told me his father was a man
of the cloth. I didn't know
what that meant to him
or what it was supposed
to mean to me. I put his cock
in my mouth; he went home
anyway. Soon after,
he quit the coffee shop
and got a job landscaping
and I didn't see him again.
Now, I hear, he teaches
English at a Catholic school
in the suburbs. He was
so lovely when he was a boy.

PETIT MAL, PETIT MORT

Latchkey. Cold as coals raked
after a fire—that's me—Betty Crocker's
demented cousin. There's nothing here,
but I am here. Watch me. I stuff my face
'cause I'm empty. Where I'm from boys and girls
fuck young, wait for the snow to go then lay
their bodies out beneath the pines to play
at *petit mal* (or is that *petit mort*?): some white fox
with a kink in her tail—then winter comes to hide
the evidence. You can get a cake from the supermarket
for $9.99 and eat the icing off with a spoon while outside
the world is white and cold. You can't get warm.
There's no one home to tell you when to sleep.

TO A FUTURE DELINQUENT

When you're a kid living on allowance
and pilfered bills, you get on the bus.
You have time to travel, feel the crush
of some frotteur's perverted glance,
furtive with desire. So what? You're young
and fetishized. You've got a pocket full
of fives. You get high and all the dull
lights of the city sing to you, strung-
out suburban wanderer out of touch,
out of town, and looking for attention.
Caution: objects in mirror are closer
than they appear slippery when wet watch
for oncoming traffic restricted vision.
All signs become apparent. All signs become clear.

B&E

A teacup, a spark plug, some hard knick-knack,
anything made of porcelain will do
the trick and knock a window out, smooth
as snow settles on a lawn. One good crack
and *shush* the glass is filigree and gold. You're in.
Linger. Run your hands across the wheel. Stop
at ten and two, check the rearview, pop
the clutch and… nothing—shit—the thing's been up on
blocks since 1982, but wait, there's still
a ton to take: AC/DC on tape,
only slightly warped, a handful of change.
The air is close and hot. Look, you can steal
a kiss in this dark car or kick the dash and take
the stereo. Decisions, decisions, decisions.

MARY HILL

Terrifying, to sit behind the wheel of the car I'd financed
with my father's blessing one Sunday afternoon, him having had

enough of shuttling me. Period. Terrifying, in that one is meant
to drive forward and always look where one is going

and me always uncertain and then certain of something larger
than myself, having imagined that sometime, almost certainly, I

wouldn't *see* anything at all: no line of cars ahead on the freeway,
no oversized inflatable hamburger buffeted in a wind atop

a fast-food franchise, no green-blue horizon or stand of cedar, just this
thank-you-and-collect-your-things *nothing*. Terrifying,

like how salvage is almost slavish, or voice is almost vice.
He'd told me "debt builds

character," meaning "get a job," so I did and drove that car
to get there. Twenty minutes to the warehouse and back, either way,

until I knew that road so well I could drive it with my eyes closed,
so I did,

some eighty kilometres an hour, ten seconds between off-ramp
and concrete divider. "Ten, nine, eight…"

NEAR MISS

I once read that people are likely to marry within a ten-mile radius of their hometown, and so I offer for your approval my high school boyfriend and his car—a Pontiac he drove religiously to the mall and back and out to a cranberry field where we'd fuck and smoke and listen to the radio most nights. I'm talking about his white-boy's hands red-knuckled and clumsy on my jeans, of parks and parking lots, the eerie shapes a playground makes against the stars. I'm talking about night, what we left behind so often in the rush before police swooped in to dump our bootleg beer, the joint we left beneath a rusted swing and the kid, next day, who found it there. Listen, I know our fumbling rose, not out of desire, but desperation. I know we drove in circles, because those were the only roads we knew. I know how it is to have a place inhabit the body, to feel a car rolling fast and a boy's hand working on your knee. We were at the mercy of location; he lived just up the street. God knows we would have loved anybody else, given the opportunity.

THE DINER OF HER HEART

never closes. Serves an all-day breakfast
to die for, pumps out that good black coffee
served by a prom-queen-cum-waitress, sexy
in her faded apron. They serve toast, crust
intact and not a cucumber in sight,
beer by the bottle: Bud or Bud or Bud,
and when the trucks pull in for love or food
the place gets hopping, guys and girls get tight
among the booths, their thighs warm the vinyl
seats until they're gone—off to make it in
the can, her pushed up against the graffiti
by the sink *sez bob wuz here jane luvs cock* while
he whispers fervent love. In the kitchen
the grease trap's burning. Everybody flees.

Drive

1

Nineteen and a half hours to drive
the first leg and, after that,
the country is mostly empty, mostly flat.
It doesn't care for us. It doesn't have
snapshots of where we pass. Our history
is silenced. Nothing to hear
but tires on this half-familiar road, nothing clear
but the recognition that I will never be
as close to those I love as I would like.
Impossible distance stretches before you.
Endless Sask., endless Man.,
endless Ont. Quebec—
You receive my sister as though
she were a seed blown on the western wind.

2

Nineteen and a half hours to drive
the stretch from Vancouver to Banff.
Two sisters in a red sedan crammed
with cassette tapes, underwear, art supplies,
a cooler filled with sandwiches, a joint
passing lazily between us as o-
ver the Coquihalla we chug lobbing
banana peels in our wake, hoisting
our bras like flags from the antenna
to flash the truckers blazing
past in their bright Mack trucks. Last
time we travelled like this we were kids, now
the road east feels both familiar and daunting,
first leg, anyway. After that?

3

For the first leg of the trip (and even after that)
Christine wears cheap shoes from Vancouver's
Chinatown. The thin black soles barely cover
her feet but she'll never throw them out
now that she's left for good. She's come
to see the country as it is, massive
and strange. In Alberta the beef cattle
blink their caramel eyes and moan
as oil pumps fuck the earth, slowly, easily.
Cowboys exist! A tractor stops to let
us pass. The driver tips his cowboy hat
and we are farmers' wives, instantly.
Who could be lonely here? Not
us on this prairie, mostly empty, mostly flat.

4

This prairie, mostly empty, mostly flat,
affords no respite from the desert heat.
My sister, who can sleep
through anything, will not drift off. She's hot,
goddammitall. She grabs a two-litre
bottle of water, chugs it down as fields
of corn and wheat shimmer past. She unfolds
the map to check out where we are:
seems like nowhere. We sing out Stompin' Tom:
"Roll on, roll on, Saskatchewan" and play at trivia
to stave off boredom. "Did you know," Chris says,
"Saskatchewan has no daylight savings?"
and I'm not surprised. What's there to save?
It doesn't care for us. It merely *stays*.

5

"I don't care what you say, it doesn't save
Third World countries to protest…" My uncle,
ex-cop, avid hunter, grips the barrel
of his rifle as he cleans it, sets us straight.
"Don't get me wrong," he says
"You have the right to say whatever you want…
but those kids at APEC weren't invited."
Christine, still recovering from the day's
drive, begins to laugh hysterically,
drinks some more of his homemade
apple wine. Regina is, as we'd forseen,
a taxidermist's dream, with all the Merry
Christmases of our childhood paraded
like snapshots of times long gone, our history.

6

Snapshots of what we've passed? Our history?
The mountains of British Columbia,
Stanley Park, the SkyTrain, suburbia.
Whole winters without snow but we could ski
Grouse Mountain or Whistler (too posh
for us, but still we'd go). Boots and T-shirts,
flip-flops (not thongs). Drunken bush parties. Dirt
ground into the knees of our jeans. Lush
sound of rain falling on the canopy
of Vancouver Island's redwood forest.
Here on the plains the Rockies seem
obscene, like lap-dancing cousins the
family would rather forget, their brazenness
silenced, so there's nothing left to hear.

7

We fall silent. Nothing to hear
at first, but then the prairie
begins to sound, sibilant as the sea-
coast of British Columbia. Our ears
are tuned now. As in a soundproof room
the rush of one's own blood is deafening,
so here grasshoppers chafe their wings
like gut-strung instruments, cello, violin,
until the whole plain feels vibrato.
We spread a red blanket on the grass.
Christine, tired of driving, has no fear
of rattlesnakes although I've told
her they live here. I wait, rapt, for the hiss
of tires on the pavement to reappear.

8

This half-familiar road, yes, this clear
wide prairie sky, the same
sky under which we were conceived and named
Elizabeth Gayle, Christine Jennifer.
Strange to see our childhood pictures
pasted into all those family scrapbooks
along the way. In Winnipeg, we look
so much like our auntie that strangers
seeing us together smile and nod as
if they know it's been a long time since we
were together. We see photos we know
well, doubles our mom must have sent
at Christmas, years ago. The shots are old,
though we see, in them, that we will never be.

9

Recognizing I may never be
the hero of my sister's life is hard.
For so long now I've tried
to be what she has never been, a keen
hard light to follow through the wrecked
house of our family—
when all I've been is another hallway,
another doorway, open or locked.
Rain begins on the yellow prairie,
unfurls itself, sighs. Christine,
beautiful, clear, cold, her mind
a scalpel's edge, has grown weary
of me. Can't read her face. Are we
closer to those we love than we would like?

10

As close to those we love as we would like—
often too close. We may have more to lose
than we can know but, Chris, unloose
your hair. In the time it takes a snake
to shed its skin, let's drive through Ontario
where we have never been,
and let's be friends. Forget that we've been
cruel, as only siblings can be. A whole
lifetime could be wasted. Let's not chance it.
Come on, this is the land of a thousand
lakes, no more parched earth, but forests
gnarled, stunted. See? Dancing
stars by the billions. Cold and bright, their
impossible distances stretch above us.

11

Impossible distances stretch before us.
Ontario, much bigger than we thought,
winds around the Great Lakes, fraught
with perilous turns and low flat rocks.
We drive into the night. All is black
outside our car but for those stars flung,
a canopy of light, across the sky. We sing
a round, like when we were kids in the back
of Mom's Volvo on the way to Lake Louise
to camp. Dad would smile, keep
us singing to pass the time, until we'd wound
our way to the campsite where we'd
pitch the tent. Then too stars gleamed,
endless, eternal as our dad and mom.

12

Endless. Endless Ont., Saskatchewan
so far behind us now it seems only
a memory. Ahead, a Chevrolet
weaves and wobbles lane to lane,
driver either drunk or near asleep. One
AM and a mist has fallen
on the forest. The trees here seem stricken
with a crippling blight, as if some
huge hand squashed them. Perhaps
the gravity here is heavier? What
an eerie place this is. Even the rocks
seem flat as if the sky had collapsed
on the earth and left it squat,
Manitoba, Ontario, Quebec.

13

Manitoba, Ontario, Quebec,
the provinces slide by our sedan
in a silent movie as if the land
itself were pulling us eastward. I don't check
the map so often now. I know we're close.
Now Christine is asleep and will not wake,
her head thrown back against
her purple travel pillow, finally lost
in dreams. Is she dreaming of Montreal
as we enter Quebec? Of streets, Saint-Urbain,
Saint-Denis, of making love in rough
weather? Ten feet of snow? *Je ne parle pas
le français*, Montreal. What a shame
my sister has to stay here now.

14

My sister has to stay in Montreal?
All right. These moves
are moves we have to make.
This is how snapshots accumulate:
think Volvo, think mosquito, think
two thousand endless miles of prairie
beige, of cattle guards and the harsh
forested Shield. O my girl,
what's next for you? You're gone
and I'm in pieces, reduced to Xmas
cards and phone calls. Look, I'm writing
like a fool, but what kind of country is this anyway,
what kind of sentence—our whole family
scattered like seeds on the western wind.

15

Like seeds blown on the western wind,
our end we've found in our beginning.
O Montreal, already you're singing
to my sister. I beg you, be good
to her, bring her lovers and friends.
Don't leave her lonely, embrace her
but, you charmer, return her to Vancouver!
We share a last coffee at departures, pretend
it's not goodbye at Dorval.
How many sisters have parted here? We are two
and trying to avoid the way Mom lives—
without her sisters. Here comes my call
to board, but Christine let go weeks ago,
I'm nineteen and a half, she said. Let's drive.

ACKNOWLEDGEMENTS

Some of these poems appeared in the following publications: *The Antigonish Review, Event, The Fiddlehead, The Malahat Review, The New Quarterly, Prairie Fire, sub-TERRAIN, Sometimes Boys Go Missing* (Mosquito Press, 2004), and *Talk That Mountain Down: Poetry from the Banff Writing Studio 2005* (littlefishcart press, 2006).

"Of a Time" is for my mom, Cathy Bachinsky; "Drive" is for my sister, Christine Bachinsky; "Wolf Lake" is for Matt Rader. Love to you all.

Although the voices in "Sometimes Boys Go Missing" are fictional, this poem was inspired by the disappearance of Maple Ridge resident Martin Balfour in 2000.

Thanks to my family and to Anar Ali, Darren Bifford, Kate Braid, Amber Dawn, Stan Dragland, Jan & Crispin Elsted, Jon Paul Fiorentino, Kuldip Gill, Bethanne Grabham, Lee Gulyas, Chris Hutchinson, Dan Kibke, Amanda Lamarche, Doretta Lau, Janey Lew, Allan MacInnis, Keith Maillard, Don McKay, George McWhirter, Jay MillAr, Gaby & Murray Morrison, Billeh Nickerson, Jada Pape, Aaron Peck, Marguerite Pigeon, Matt Rader, Kathy Sinclair, Michael V. Smith, Nick Thran, Rhea Tregebov, Russell Wangersky, Silas White, and David Zieroth for their friendship, support and editorial advice.

Thanks also to all the excellent people at The Banff Centre Writing Studio (2005); The Canada Council for the Arts, whose assistance sustained me through the editing of this manuscript; and to The Maple Ridge & Pitt Meadows Arts Council and the Ridge Meadows Parks & Leisure Services Commission, whose residency was invaluable.

And finally, thanks and love to my very own outcast, Blake Smith, for his keen ear and kind heart. Thank you.